When Polly Pratt Came to Play —

Plate 1—October 1919

— Of Course She Brought Her Doll

Plate 2—October 1919

Polly Pratt's Little Country Cousin

Plate 3—July/August 1920

Polly Pratt Had a Valentine

Plate 4—February 1920

Every Girl Should Have One—Maybe Two or Three

Plate 5—February 1920

Polly Pratt Gave a May Day Party and Betty Brown Rode Over on Her Pony

Plate 6—May 1920

Polly Pratt Goes to a Vacation Camp and Meets Janey Taylor

Plate 7—June 1920

Polly Pratt's New Friends at School

Plate 8—September 1920

Polly Pratt Gives a Hallowe'en Party

Plate 9—October 1920

Polly Pratt's Christmas Caller

Plate 10—December 1920

Polly's Neighbors Come to Play

Plate 11—January 1921

Polly Gives a Fancy Dress Party

Plate 12—February 1921

Polly Pratt's Easter Visitors

Plate 13—April 1921

Polly Pratt Gives a Doll Party

Plate 14—May 1921

Polly Has a Fourth of July Picnic

Plate 15—July 1921

Polly Visits Friends at the Seashore

Plate 16—August 1921